A WHO'S WHO OF THE MANSON FAMILY

A WHO'S WHO OF THE MANSON FAMILY

Adam Gorightly &
Shamus McFarland

feejeepress.com

A Who's Who of the Manson Family
Copyright © 2010 by Adam Gorightly
All rights reserved. No part of this book may be
used or reproduced in any manner whatsoever without
prior written permission except in the case of brief
quotations embodied in critical articles or reviews.
For information visit the author's website at
adamgorightly.com.

Cover design by Shamus McFarland

First Print Edition 2011

Feejee Press
feejeepress.com

ISBN 1456585010
ISBN-13: 978-1456585013

The opinions expressed in this book are the author's and do not represent those of the publisher. The author has sought permission for the use of all illustrations and substantial quotations known by him to be in copyright. Any omissions should be brought to the attention of the author.

Contents & Characters

INTRODUCTION: The Thing That Refused To Die / xiii

ALONZO, Maria Therasa / 1

ANDREWS, Claudia / 1

ATKINS, Susan Denise / 2

BAILEY, Edward Arthur / 5

BAILEY, Ella Jo / 5

BAILEY, Lawrence / 6

BAKER, David Ralph / 7

BALDWIN, Linda / 7

BARABAS, Edward / 7

BARTELL, Susan Phyllis / 8

BEAUSOLEIL, Robert Kenneth / 8

BO; see ROSENBERG, Barbara / 11

BOBBY; see BEAUSOLEIL, Robert / 11

BOMSE, Robert Michael / 11

BRENDA; see PITMAN, Nancy / 11

BROOKS; see POSTON, Brooks / 12

BROWN, Kenneth Richard / 12

BRUCE / 12

BRUNNER, Mary Theresa / 12

CAFRITZ, Charlene / 15

CAPPY / 15

CHUCKLEBERRY / 16

CLEM / 16

COLE, William Rex / 16

COMO, Kenneth Daniel / 17

COOPER, Priscilla Kay / 18

COOPER, Sherry Ann / 18

COTTAGE, Madaline Joan / 19

COUNTRY SUE / 19

COVELL, Louis Charles / 20

CRAIG, James Terrill / 20

CRAVENS, Larry / 21

CRAZY PATTY / 21

CROCKETT, Paul / 21

CROWE, Bernard / 22

CUPID / 23

DANNY / 25

DAVIS, Bruce McGregor / 25

DAVIS, Scotty / 26

DeCARLO, Daniel Thomas / 26

86 GEORGE / 29

FLYNN, John Leo / 31

FREIDMAN, John / 31

FROMME, Lynette Alice / 32

GENTRY, Jennifer Sue / 35

GILLIES, Catherine Irene / 35

GOOD, Sandra Collins / 36

GOUCHER, William / 37

GROGAN, Steve Dennis / 38

GYPSY / 38

HAMIC, David / 41

HANNUM, David / 41

HAUGHT, John Philip / 42

HAY, Misty / 43

HINMAN, Gary / 44

HOYT, Barbara / 44

JAKOBSON, Gregg / 47

JONES, Larry / 47

JUAN / 47

JUANITA / 47

KASABIAN, Linda Darlene Drouin / 49

KATIE / 50

KAUFMAN, Phillip Clark / 51

KITTY / 51

KRENWINKEL, Patricia / 52

LAKE, Diane Elizabeth / 55

LANE, Robert Ivan / 56

LANSBURY, Deidre / 56

LEGHORN, Jennifer / 57

LESLIE / 57

LINDA / 57

LIPSETT, David William / 58

LITTLE LARRY / 58

LITTLE PATTY / 58

LOVETT, Charles / 59

LUTESINGER, Katherine Rene / 59

MANSON, Charles Milles / 61

MELCHER, Terry / 67

MELTON, Charles / 68

MELTON, Larry Allen / 68

MCCANN, Brenda / 69

MONFORT, Michael Lee / 69

MONTGOMERY, Charles / 69

MOOREHOUSE, Deane Allen / 70

MOOREHOUSE, Ruth Ann / 71

MORGLEA, Randy J. / 71

MURRAY, Robert Earl / 72

OUISH/OUISCH / 75

PIERCE, Charles / 77

PITMAN, Nancy Laura / 77

PLUMLEE, Vernon Ray Dean / 78

POSTON, Brooks Ramsey / 79

PUGH, Joel / 80

RAPH, Kevin Schooler / 83

RICE, Dennis / 83

ROSENBERG, Barbara / 84

ROSS, Mark Stephen / 85

ROUGH, Johnny Kevin / 85

ROWE, Stephanie Gale / 86

SADIE / 89

SANDY / 89

SCHRAM, Stephanie Jean / 89

SCHWARM, Mary Ann / 90

SCOTT, Suzanne / 90

SCOTTY / 90

SHARE, Catherine Louise / 91

SHEA, Donald Jerome / 92

SHEPPARD, Laura Ann / 93

SIMI VALLEY SHERRY / 93

SINCLAIR, Colleen Ann / 94

SINDER, Ella Beth / 94

SMITH, Claudia Leigh / 94

SNAKE / 95

SOUPSPOON / 95

SQUEAKY / 95

STEPHANIE / 95

TEX / 97

TJ / 97

TODD, Hugh Rocky / 97

TOWNSEND, Herb / 97

TRACEY, Beth / 97

TRUE, Harold Irving / 98

VAN HOUTEN, Leslie Louise / 101

VERN / 102

VON AHN, Diane / 102

WALLACE, Kay / 105

WALLEMAN, Tom / 105

WALTS, Allen / 106

WALTS, Mark / 106

WARTHAN, Perry / 106

WATKINS, Paul Allen / 107

WATSON, Charles Denton / 108

WILD, Victor Floyd / 109

WILDEBUSH, Joan / 109

WILLETT, James L. / 110

WILLETT, Lauren Chavelle Olmstead / 110

WILSON, Dennis Carl / 111

YELLER / 115

ZERO / 117

About the Authors / 119

Companion Soundtrack / 120

INTRODUCTION:
The Thing That Refused To Die

This book's evolution has gone through several iterations, beginning with Shamus McFarland's initial stab (pun intended) that appeared in *Cyberculture Counterconspiracy: A Steamshovel Press Web Reader, Volume 2* (Book Tree, 2000).

Afterwards—in cahoots with Mr. McFarland—I expanded upon his original version, including it as an appendix to my tome *The Shadow Over Santa Susana: Black Magic, Mind Control and the Manson Family Mythos* (iUniverse, 2001).

In 2009, when a deal was inked with Creation Books to revise *The Shadow Over Santa Susana*, I decided to breathe life anew into the 'ol *Who's Who*, dusting off those creepy crawly cobwebs and adding new material for inclusion in the revised Creation Books edition. However, and much to my chagrin, Creation—for whatever reason—opted not to use this new *Who's Who* and so it languished until early 2010 at which time Feejee Press stepped forward with interest in the project, both in the traditional print version format and as a virtual e-book. To this end, I immediately got busy with yet another rewrite to document recent developments that had transpired in the wacky world of Charlie Manson and his legion of former Family members. And that—in a nutshell—explains the nasty little beast you now hold in your hands.

Without further ado, I give you, dear readers, the latest and greatest, revised and revamped, fun-filled and blood curdling rendition of *A Who's Who of the Manson Family* for your possible reading enjoyment.

Adam Gorightly — July 2010.

ALONZO, Maria Therasa
Nickname: Crystal
DOB: 1952
AKA: Forbes, Karen Marie

Maria Alonzo—an X carved on her head—was among a group of Manson Family leftovers renting a house on West Flora Street in Stockton, California during the early 1970s. This West Flora gang included Nancy Pitman, Priscilla Cooper, and three Aryan Brotherhood members: Michael Lee Monfort, James (Spider) Craig, and William (Iceman/Chilly Willy) Goucher. Lauren and James Willett—who also lived at the West Flora address—were later found murdered.

Alonzo married William Goucher on February 15th, 1973. In 1974, Alonzo was sentenced to six months in jail for taking part in a failed plot to kidnap a foreign diplomat.

ANDREWS, Claudia; see SMITH, Claudia
Page 94

ATKINS, Susan Denise
DOB: 5-7-48
Nickname: Sexy Sadie, Violet
AKA: Glutz, Sadie Mae; King, Sharon; Powell, Donna Kay

In 1966, Anton LaVey—High Priest of the Church of Satan—formed a topless go-go dance troupe that performed in San Francisco's North Beach featuring Susan Atkins in the role of "The Vampire." Photos from the period show Atkins wearing an open black robe revealing her nude body, mock blood dripping from her lips. Three years later, Atkins confessed to licking the blood from the knife used to kill Sharon Tate, as her vampire fantasy became gruesome reality.

When Atkins was taken into custody for the Hinman murder, she reveled in her memories of the Cielo Drive murders, confessing to cellmates Ronnie Howard and Virginia Graham that it was the best sexual experience of her life. Atkins initially struck a deal with the prosecution that spared her from the death penalty. She testified at the grand jury proceeding, which led to indictments against the other defendants, including Manson, but later backed out of the deal and refused to testify. The prosecution turned to Linda Kasabian and struck a deal for her testimony, and Atkins was convicted on one count of conspiracy to murder and seven counts of first-degree murder. She received the death penalty, but her sentence was reduced to life when California repealed the death penalty in 1972.

While in prison, Atkins' was twice married. Her first nuptial, in 1981, to Donald "Flash" Laisure—who at fifty-six was nineteen years her senior—was short-lived. On an episode of *Geraldo*, Laisure recounted an incident where Atkins attempted to shank him during a conjugal visit, pulling up his shirt to display a horizontal cut running across his stomach. Atkins remarried in 1987 to James Whitehouse, a law school graduate fifteen years her junior, to whom she was married to up until the time of her death.

In July 2008, officials at Corona Women's Prison made a compassionate release request due to Atkins' deteriorating condition, which included the loss of a leg and unsuccessful surgery for brain cancer. However, Atkins' request was denied, a move supported by Governor Arnold Schwarzenegger.

Atkins was last incarcerated at the Central California Women's Facility in Chowchilla, California, in a skilled nursing unit, where she passed away on September 24th, 2009.

BAILEY, Edward Arthur
AKA: Bailey, Ed

Introduced to the Manson Family by Bill Vance and Vern Plumlee. Bailey claimed that he saw Manson shoot a guy in the head with a .45 automatic at Barker Ranch.

BAILEY, Ella Jo
Nickname: Yeller, Yellerstone
AKA: Sinder, Ella Beth; Simpson, Ella; Jackson, Susan Ann; Powell, Martha

An early Manson Family member, Danny DeCarlo once described Bailey as a sultry Greta Garbo type.

Beach Boy Dennis Wilson picked up Ella Jo and Patricia Krenwinkel hitchhiking and took them back to his Sunset Boulevard pad to show off his gold records and fuck. This was how Manson discovered where Wilson lived, and a short time afterwards Charlie invited himself and the girls to Wilson's house one evening when the Beach Boy was at an all night recording session. Early the next morning, Wilson arrived home to find a gaggle of half naked girls in his living room dancing to tunes on his hi-fi set and drinking all his liquor, thus beginning Wilson's courtship with Charlie and his troupe.

Ella Jo split in fear from Spahn Ranch—prior to the Tate-LaBianca murders—when Susan Atkins revealed her role in the Hinman murder.

BAILEY, Lawrence
DOB: 10-20-49 or 10-12-49
POB: Tulsa, OK / Kaiserslaughter, Germany
Nickname: Little Larry
AKA: Jones, Larry; Bailey, Lawrence Charles

A part-time wrangler, Bailey was arrested at both Spahn Ranch and Barker Ranch raids and for the Western Surplus Store robbery. Bailey was allegedly involved in Shorty Shea's murder.

BAKER, David Ralph
DOB: 8-3-46 or 2-9-50
Nickname: Karate Dave
AKA: Lipsett, David William; Ellis, Charles; Lipsick, David

A Vietnam vet recruited into the Family by Charlie. Baker hooked up with Bo Rosenberg at the Yellow Submarine house, and lived with her in a tree-house in the backyard of the property.

BALDWIN, Linda; see Cottage, Madaline Joan
Page 19

BARABAS, Edward
DOB: 1951
AKA: Ekron Chad Skeens

After being released from Folsom Prison, Barabas was living with Manson follower Priscilla Cooper in Sacramento in the late 1970's. In November of '78, Barabas was found murdered and stuffed into the trunk of a burning car along with another Manson Family associate, one James "Spider" Craig, who had been shot in the face, but survived.

BARTELL, Susan Phyllis
DOB: 6-28-51
Nickname: Country Sue

Arrested with Family members in the Barker Ranch raid. With John "Zero" Haught when he died. Bartell faded from the Family scene in the mid-70's.

BEAUSOLEIL, Robert Kenneth
DOB: 11-6- 47
Nicknames: Jase, Jasper; Bobby, Cherub, Cupid
AKA: Hardey, Robert Lee; Daniels, Jason Lee
Prison I.D.# B 28302

As a teen, Beausoleil was involved in the Los Angeles music scene, playing guitar in an early version of Arthur Lee's Love. He later landed a role in the exploitation film *Mondo Hollywood* that also featured future Manson Family murder victim Jay Sebring. In late

1965, Beausoleil moved to San Francisco and formed a band called The Orkustra that played the first Golden Gate Park concert, along with The Grateful Dead. During this period, Beausoleil worked with experimental film director, Kenneth Anger, on a project titled *Lucifer Rising*, footage that was later used in Anger's *Invocation for my Demon Brother*, also featuring Anton LaVey. During this period, Beausoleil lived with Anger at his house in the Haight Ashbury, home to the former Russian Embassy. Beausoleil and Anger eventually had a falling out when the director claimed that Bobby had stolen the original *Lucifer Rising* film footage, inspiring Anger to place a curse on his young protégé.

After breaking with Anger, Beausoleil formed a short-lived group called The Devil's Band that played some gigs around Berkeley before he split the Bay Area and moved to L.A.'s Topanga Canyon in the fall of '67. At this time, Beausoleil appeared in a soft-core sexploitation Western called *Ramrodder* and during the shooting met future Manson Family member Catherine "Gypsy" Share, who also had a role in the film.

In early 1968, Beausoleil met Charlie Manson and some of his girls singing together at an old Gothic Mansion in Topanga Canyon known as "The Spiral Staircase." Afterwards, Charlie and the girls stayed with Bobby at his Topanga Canyon pad, and it was during this time that he and Manson formed a six-piece electric rock band dubbed The Milky Way, with Charlie on guitar and Bobby on guitar and bass clarinet. The band was short-lived, though it did have one weekend of public performances at the Topanga Corral.

During the Topanga Canyon period, Beausoleil associated with Gary Hinman, a bathtub chemist and drug dealer, who Bobby served as a middleman for, peddling mescaline. When a drug deal went south with The Satan's Slaves biker gang, Beausoleil tried to get the gang their money back, but Hinman refused to return the cash. This ultimately led to a standoff, which resulted in Beausoleil stabbing Hinman to death on July 27th, 1969, the first official Manson Family murder.

On August 4th, Beausoleil was arrested in San Luis Obispo, sleeping on the side of Highway 1 in Hinman's stolen Fiat. During Beausoleil's arrest, the police found the murder weapon—a thunderbird knife, stained with Hinman's blood—in the wheel well of the vehicle. Bobby was taken into custody and charged with murder. On April 18th, 1970, he was found guilty of 1st degree murder and sentenced to death.

In the early 1970's, Led Zeppelin guitarist Jimmy Page was working on the soundtrack for a new version of Kenneth Anger's *Lucifer Rising*. However, Anger and Page had a falling out and the soundtrack for the film was eventually recorded in prison by Beausoleil, who had reconciled with Anger. The soundtrack evolved out of jam sessions with other Tracy Prison players, including former Family member, Steve Grogan.

Throughout his forty years in prison, Beausoleil—currently incarcerated at the Oregon State Penitentiary—has continued producing music. In 2004, Beausoleil's *Lucifer Rising* soundtrack was re-released. Other CD releases include *Running With The White*

Wolf (1998) and *Dreamways of the Mystic* (2006.)

In 1982, Beausoleil met and married his wife, Barbara.

BO; see ROSENBERG, Barbara

Page 84

BOBBY; see BEAUSOLEIL, Robert

Page 8

BOMSE, Robert Michael

Mentioned in Sanders' *The Family*. Arrested for Marijuana and LSD with Susan Atkins, Mary Brunner, Stephanie Rowe, Patricia Krenwinkel and Ella Jo Bailey.

BRENDA; see PITMAN, Nancy

Page 77

BROOKS; see POSTON, Brooks
Page 79

BROWN, Kenneth Richard
AKA: Scott Bell Davis; Scotty, Crebs

John "Zero" Haught's friend from Ohio. Arrested during the Barker Ranch raid. Danny DeCarlo told investigators that Scotty and Zero were two boys who had joined Charlie's Family, but didn't fit in. They hadn't been with the Family very long before Zero was murdered/committed suicide.

BRUCE; see DAVIS, Bruce
Page 25

BRUNNER, Mary Theresa
DOB: 12-17-43
POB: Eau Claire, WI
Nickname: Mother Mary, Marioche
AKA: Manson, Mary Theresa; Moser, Lynda Lee; Euchts, Christine Marie; Och, Mary

After Manson's 1967 Terminal Island release, Mary met Charlie when he was hanging around the Berkeley campus library where she worked. Brunner is generally considered to be the first Manson Family member. She was in jail for forgery during the Spahn Ranch raid and then released on September 3rd, 1969. Involved in the August 27th, 1971 Western Surplus Store shootout, Brunner received two consecutive ten years-to-life sentences. Released on parole, she returned to her family home in Wisconsin where she raised Charlie Manson's son.

CAFRITZ, Charlene

In December 1968, Charlie and three of his girls visited a private dude ranch in Reno, Nevada where they were guests of a wealthy divorcee, Charlene Cafritz, whom Manson had met earlier that summer at Dennis Wilson's house. Cafritz—who had been awarded nearly two million dollars in a divorce settlement—blew the entire sum in a spending spree over the course of ten months, often aided by Charlie.

Apparently, Cafritz—who just happened to be good friends with Sharon Tate and Terry Melcher—took numerous motion pictures of Charlie and the girls in Reno that have since become shrouded in silence. The police learned about Cafritz from Gregg Jakobson, and eventually traced her to St. Elizabeths Mental Hospital in Washington, D.C.

On August 11th, 1970—during the course of the Tate/LaBianca trial—Cafritz called Spahn Ranch from St. Elizabeths and informed certain Family members that she possessed tapes and photos unknown to the police. On September 4th, Cafritz died of an accidental overdose of Nembutol and these alleged films of the Family never surfaced.

CAPPY; see GILLIES, Catherine

Page 35

CHUCKLEBERRY; see LOVETT, Charles

Page 59

CLEM; see GROGAN, Steve Davis

Page 38

COLE, William Rex
(Known as Bill Vance)
DOB: 4-17-35
Nicknames: Duane; Bill; Buck; Vance; Chuck
AKA: Vance, William Joseph; Hamic, David Lee; Vansickle, William Joseph; Vansickle, Billy; Schwarm, Duane

One of Charlie's ex-con recruits, Cole arranged for Susan Atkins, Ella Jo Bailey, Stephanie Rowe, Patricia Krenwinkel and Mary Brunner to work as topless dancers. He also took Tex and some of the girls out on their first creepy-crawl dry run, teaching them how to remove screens, slip locks, avoid watchdogs, and implement the tools of the trade, such as penknives, razor blades, bobby pins, and pieces of wire. A talented lock picker, Cole helped Manson and his bunch break into a Mulholland mansion belonging to the rock group Iron Butterfly when Manson learned the band was out of town for a few weeks.

Cole was arrested during the Barker Ranch raid and later relocated to northern Missouri in 1972.

COMO, Kenneth Daniel
DOB: 1940
DOD: September 2004
Nickname: Curly
AKA: Jones, Jesse

Led the Western Surplus Store robbery. Arrested, escaped October 20th, 1971 and recaptured when Sandy Good crashed the getaway vehicle. Como was sentenced fifteen years to life. While in prison he joined the Aryan Brotherhood, and attempted another escape on December 13th, 1974. Como married Catherine Share in 1977 during incarceration.

COOPER, Priscilla Kay
DOB: 8-19-51
Nickname: Tuffy
AKA: Edwards, Cathy

Arrested with Nancy Pitman and Squeaky Fromme in November 1972 in Stockton, California, in possession of an auto that belonged to murder victims James and Lauren Willett. Cooper pled guilty to murder-accessory after the fact in the Willett murders.

COOPER, Sherry Ann
DOB: 5-17-49
Possibly 8-1-49 (Spahn raid) or 5-19-52
POB: TN
AKA: Simi Valley Sherri; Sherry, Ruthie; Heuvelhurst, Ruth Ann

Arrested during the Spahn Ranch raid. Fled Barker Ranch with

Barbara Hoyt (or Bo Rosenberg, depending on the source), then went to stay with Danny DeCarlo in Venice Beach.

COTTAGE, Madaline Joan
DOB: 5-27-46
Nicknames: Patty; Little Patty, Crazy Patty
AKA: Baldwin, Linda Loju; McCoy, Shirley Amanda; Baldwin, Patricia Joan

Arrested with the Manson Family at both ranch raids. In bedroom with John "Zero" Haught when he died.

COUNTRY SUE; see BARTELL, Susan

COVELL, Louis Charles
DOB: 10-16-44
POB: Long Beach, CA
Nickname: A-1

Unknown, arrested with the Family.

CRAIG, James Terrill
DOB: 1939
Nickname: Spider

Aryan Brotherhood member and Manson Family associate in the 1970's. Pled guilty as accessory after the fact in the 1972 Willett murders. In November of '78, Craig—who had been shot in the face—was discovered in the trunk of a burning car in Sacramento, California, along with the slain body of another Manson Family associate, Edward Barabas. Both Barabas and Craig had been recently released from Folsom Prison at the time of this incident, which authorities suspected of being a prison gang related hit. As he was being transported to Sacramento University Medical Center, Craig repeatedly said, "She's dangerous... she's dangerous..."

CRAVENS, Larry
DOB: 3-20-40
AKA: Little Larry Jones

A Spahn Ranch hand arrested in Spahn raid.

CRAZY PATTY; see COTTAGE, Madaline
Page 19

CROCKETT, Paul

A miner who associated with Manson Family members in Death Valley. Crockett "deprogrammed" Family members Paul Watkins, Brooks Poston and Juanita Wildebush, and provided asylum for Juan Flynn after he broke from Manson. Crockett testified for the Tate/LaBianca prosecution. Currently, Crockett lives in Washington State and bills himself as a "Transformational Counseler."

CROWE, Bernard
DOB: 4-13-42
DOD: 2-1-93
AKA: Lotsa Poppa

Crowe lived at 7008 Woodrow Wilson Drive near Sunset at a house well known for sun deck sex scenes and conspicuous dope dealing. According to Ed Sanders, Manson and some associates were often seen hanging out around Woodrow Wilson and Loyal Trail, a short road that ran behind Crowe's place, and it is probable that Charlie and his gang were either visiting Crowe's house or, according to other sources, Mama Cass Elliot's place located nearby. One former Family member has stated that in late 1968 some Family members used to visit a "Bernie's house" in the Laurel Canyon-Woodrow Wilson area, and Dianne Lake once referred to Crowe as "the Negro member of the Family."

In the summer of 1969, Tex Watson ripped off Crowe for $2000 in a drug burn. When Crowe took Watson's girlfriend—Rosina Kroner—hostage at her apartment, Manson showed up and shot Crowe in the gut, leaving him for dead.

Crowe survived the shooting and later testified for the Tate/LaBianca prosecution.

CUPID; see BEAUSOLEIL, Bobby

Page 8

DANNY; see DeCARLO, Daniel
Page 26

DAVIS, Bruce McGregor
DOB: 10-5-42 or 10-25-42
POB: Monroe, LA
AKA: Davis, George McGregor; McMilliam, Jack Paul; McGregor, Bruce; McMillian, Bruce; McMillan, Jack Paul
Prisoner I.D.# B 41079

One of the first male members of Charlie's gang, Davis was editor of his high school yearbook in Kingston, Tennessee, and attended the University of Tennessee for three years before "dropping out" and joining the Family in late 1967.

In February 1970, Davis was indicted for the Hinman murder and promptly disappeared. Accompanied by Nancy Pitman, Davis turned himself in to authorities in December 1970. He received two life sentences for the Hinman and Shea murders.

Davis was born again in 1973 and while in prison married and fathered a child. In a 1993 parole trasncript, he implicated Lawrence Bailey and Bill Vance in the Shorty Shea murder.

DAVIS, Scotty; see BROWN, Kenneth

Page 12

DeCARLO, Daniel Thomas
DOB: 6-20-44
POB: Arizona
Nickname: Danny, Donkey Dan, Donkey Dick
AKA: Reynolds, Danny Frederick; Romeo, Daniel; Romo, Daniel; Smith, Richard Allen; Bell, Danny Thomas

Arrested during the Spahn Ranch raid, DeCarlo—a member of the Straight Satans biker gang—met the Manson Family in Canoga Park at the Yellow Submarine house, then later moved to Spahn's to fix Dune buggies. He stayed, he said, because of all the pretty chicks. DeCarlo later told authorities that his rapport with Manson was enhanced by the fact that he could sexually satisfy the Family girls, thus taking the pressure off Charlie to keep them all happy. Because of this, Danny acquired the nickname of "Donkey Dan", a tribute to the size of his you-know-what.

DeCarlo was the official Manson Family gunsmith. His father had sold firearms for a living, and from pops Danny learned the tricks of the trade, having dismantled, repaired and fired all kinds of weapons. At Spahn Ranch, DeCarlo set up a small munitions factory in the "Undertaker's Parlor" on the Western ranch set, which they renamed the gunroom.

DeCarlo's information to investigators helped Bugliosi charge Manson with murder.

86 GEORGE

Manson paid a traffic ticket for 86 George—President of The Straight Satans motorcycle gang—in exchange for a homemade two-foot razor sharp weapon with a knuckle-guard, which Manson thereafter dubbed his "Ceremonial Sword." Charlie would use this very same blade to sacrifice Gary Hinman's ear to the gods of Helter Skelter. Later, several Straight Satans members visited Spahn Ranch to collect the sword, then afterwards dismantled it and buried its parts on the grounds of their Venice Beach clubhouse.

FLYNN, John Leo
DOB: 11-9-43
POB: Panama
AKA: Flynn, John Lee; Juan Flynn

A Vietnam vet, Flynn worked at Spahn's as a wrangler and was arrested with the Family during the Spahn Ranch raid. In early September 1969, Flynn broke off from Manson and lived with Paul Watkins, Brooks Poston and Paul Crockett in Death Valley.

FREIDMAN, John

Twelve-year-old boy arrested during the Spahn Ranch raid. The son of an artist that lived at the ranch before the Manson Family arrived.

FROMME, Lynette Alice
DOB: 10-22-48
POB: Santa Monica
Nickname: Squeaky, Red
AKA: Fromme, Lynn Alice; Williamson, Elizabeth Alaine

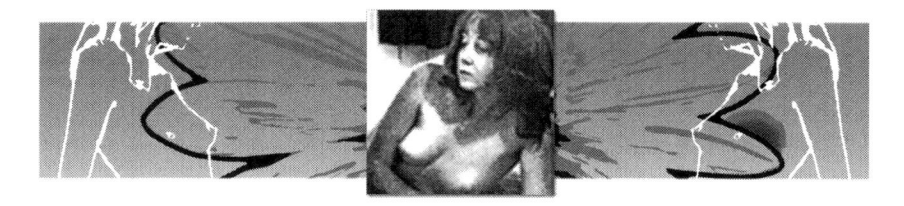

In 1967, Charlie brought Lynette home to meet Mary Brunner after he found the future "Squeaky" crying on a street corner after being thrown out of her father's place in Redondo Beach. Thus, Mary and Squeaky were the first two girls of Manson's gang.

At the California State Capital in September 1975, Fromme pulled a Colt .45 on then President Gerald Ford that failed to fire. At the time, she was living in Sacramento with Sandy Good where the two were waging a radical campaign to bust Charlie out of prison. During this period, the girls belonged to a new religious order Manson had cooked up called the Order of the Rainbow.

After her 1975 conviction for President Ford's attempted assassination, Fromme was sentenced to life in prison. On December 23rd, 1987—serving a life sentence at West Virginia's Alderson prison—Fromme was reported missing, and a nationwide alert went out as security was stepped up for ex-President Ford. On Christmas Day, Fromme was apprehended in the woods near Alderson and subsequently transferred to Lexington, Kentucky with fifteen months added to her sentence. Reportedly, Squeaky's escape was motivated by a false rumor that Charlie was dying of testicular cancer, which prompted an overwhelming desire to see her groovy little guru one last time.

On August 14th, 2009—just a few days after the 40th anniversary of the Manson Family slayings—Fromme was released on parole from the Federal Medical Center, Carswell in Fort Worth, Texas and has reportedly relocated to Marcy, New York.

GENTRY, Jennifer Sue
DOB: 3-17-48
POB: Santa Monica
Nickname: Jennie
AKA: Leghorn, Jennifer Sue; Leghorn, Jennifer S.

Captioned as Jennifer Leghorn in the 1970 documentary *Manson*. Captioned as "Ginny Gentry" in *Life* Magazine, 1970. Joined Charlie's Family after the Tate/LaBianca arrests.

GILLIES, Catherine Irene
DOB: 8-2-49
POB: Santa Cruz, CA
Nicknames: Patty Ann; Cathy; Cappy; Capistrano
AKA: Burke, Patricia Ann; Worrell, December Elaine; Jardin, Pattie; Meyers, Cathy

A former Buffalo Springfield groupie, Gillies joined around August

1968 and was arrested with the Family at both ranch raids. Her grandmother, Arlene Barker, owned Myers Ranch. It was said that Manson sent people to kill Mrs. Barker, but they were foiled by a flat tire.

Gillies real name may be Cathy Myers. She raised children in California and at one point was working as a motel housekeeper. In the late 1990's, Gillies/Myers appeared in a video filmed at Barker Ranch by researcher Bill Nelson.

GOOD, Sandra Collins
DOB: 2-20-44
POB: San Diego/Hollywood
Nicknames: Sandy; Blue
AKA: Pugh, Sandra Collins; Collins, Sandra

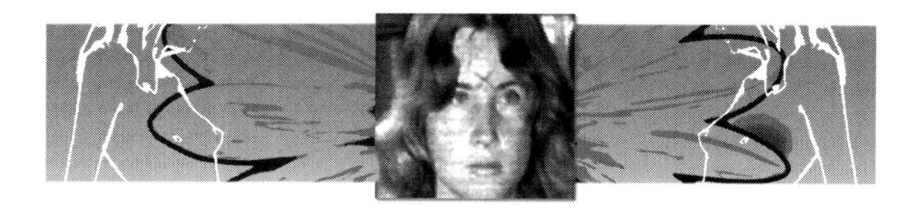

The daughter of a San Diego stockbroker, and a former San Francisco State College student, she is listed as Sandra Pugh in the earliest reports, although Good denies ever being married to Joel Pugh, who was found dead in a London hotel in December 1969.

In 1976, Good was convicted of conspiracy to mail threatening letters. Sentenced to fifteen years, she served ten. Good began her sentence at FCI - Terminal Island, California, and was later transferred to FCI - Pleasanton, and finally to FCI - Alderson. Since she aided in the 1971 prison escape of Kenneth Como, Good is prohibited from entering a State Prison again, at least as a visitor. In 1996, Good and her boyfriend, George Stimson, launched ATWA, a website offering information about Manson's purported unfair treatment by the authorities, as well as his involvement in environmental activism. At this time, Good moved to Hanford, California, located in close proximity to Charlie at Corcoran State Prison.

In 2001, the site went offline. At that time, Good left Hanford and has since issued no further statements in support of Manson or ATWA. Rumor has it Manson ended their relationship.

GOUCHER, William
DOB: 1949
Nicknames: Chilly Willy, Iceman

A Family associate in the 1970's. Pled guilty to 2nd degree in the murder of James Willett and received five years to life. Married Maria Alonzo.

GROGAN, Steve Dennis

DOB: 7-13-51
POB: San Francisco
Nicknames: Scramblehead; Clem; Gary
AKA: Dennis Tufts, Garth; Glarehouse, Clemmons; Tufts, Gary; Whitaker, Steve; Grogan, Steven; Mollan, Grant

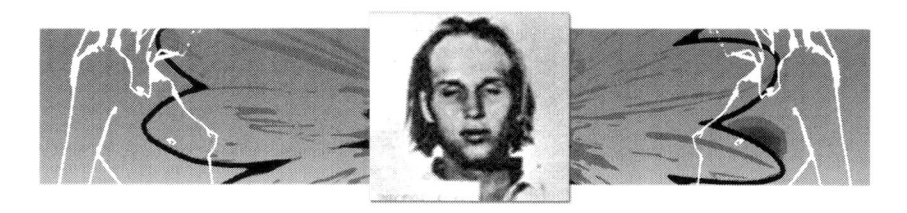

Convicted in the Shorty Shea murder. In 1977, Grogan cooperated with authorities by revealing the location of Shea's buried remains at Spahn Ranch. This disclosure helped Grogan secure his parole and to date he's the only Family member convicted of murder who has been released. Since then, Grogan has been involved in the music industry, and at one time reportedly toured with Hank Williams, Jr. Recently, Grogan has been using the stage name Adam Gabriel and has been performing in two bands that have released albums: Rhythmtown-Jive and Christmas Jug Band. The latter provided a song used in a Christmas episode of the TV sitcom *My Name is Earl*.

GYPSY; see SHARE, Catherine

Page 91

HAMIC, David; see Cole, William Rex

Page 16

HANNUM, David
DOB: 1-8-49

A Spahn Ranch hand, arrested during the Spahn Ranch raid, Hannum occasionally lent his car to the Family. It was this same car that Linda Kasabian abandoned in Albuquerque when she fled. Tex Watson and Diane Lake were staying at Hannum's ranch in Olancha when the Spahn raid went down. On August 18th, 1969, Snake Lake was arrested at Hannum's place for nude sunbathing.

HAUGHT, John Philip
DOB: 4-20-47
POB: Joplin, MO / Steubenville, Ohio
DOD: 11-5-69
Nickname: Zero
AKA: Jesus, Christopher

John Philip Haught was arrested during the Barker Ranch raid and then released with Bruce Davis in late October 1969.

On November 5th, 1969, a suicide call was placed from a beach house in Venice, California. When police arrived, they discovered Haught on a mattress in a bedroom with a fatal bullet lodged in his head. According to those present—Manson Family members Bruce Davis, Madeline Cottage, Cathy Gillies and Sue Bartell—Haught had been playing Russian roulette, and lost. But unlike the traditional method of the game—with one bullet in the chamber—Haught was playing with all chambers loaded, except one. At the time, officers present at the scene were unaware that Inyo County authorities following the Barker Ranch raid had recently released the three witnesses who observed Haught allegedly blow his brains out.

Although Haught's death appeared suspicious, police ruled it suicide, and officially closed the case. Author Ed Sanders—during the period he was hanging out with the Family at Spahn's—learned that Haught had been considered a "weak link" who some felt might rat out Charlie and the girls. Rumor has it, Haught was having sex with one or more of the girls present at the Venice Beach house when his life was snuffed out, and he truly became "Zero".

HAY, Misty
AKA: Gillum, Pat

A young woman named Misty Hay began corresponding with Manson in 1976 and, in due time, was arrested and sentenced to five years in the federal pen for sending threatening letters through the U.S. Postal Service. In September of '76, Hay sent a signed death threat to the president of the Sierra Club stating that "Charles Manson has people watching you now... so do your part to stop them from cutting down trees, or else you'll be chopped up yourselves. For every tree you let be cut down, you shall have your limbs cut off. Take heed of this mean letter or die!"

HINMAN, Gary
DOB: 12-24-34
DOD: 7-27-69

A music teacher and drug dealer who befriended Charlie's Family and occasionally allowed them to crash at his pad. Found murdered; stabbed four times. "Political Piggy" was scrawled on the wall in the victim's blood. Bobby Beausoleil was apprehended driving Hinman's car with a knife, bloody shirt and trousers in the vehicle.

HOYT, Barbara
DOB: 12-27-51
POB: Washington, D.C.
AKA: Whyer, Barbara; Lipsett, Barbara Jeanne

Identified as Barbara Rosenberg in Bugliosi's *Helter Skelter*, although Hoyt and Rosenberg were two different people. Hoyt joined the Family in April 1969. She was arrested at Spahn Ranch, but fled before the Barker Ranch raid, returning to her parents who prompted her to contact the authorities in late '69.

On September 5th, 1970—during the Tate/LaBianca trial—Hoyt left her parents' home after receiving a phone call from Manson Family members. Shortly after, she and Ruth Ann Moorehouse flew to Hawaii where they stayed a few days in a motel. It was there that Moorehouse laced Hoyt's hamburger with ten hits of acid and then abandoned her, taking a plane back to the states. A good samaritan helped the tripping Barbara from the Honolulu street and her father returned her to Los Angeles where she later testified for the prosecution. Bugliosi last heard that she was studying nursing when he published *Helter Skelter*. Born Again, Hoyt was tracked down in 2000 by Manson researcher Bill Nelson. At that time, she was allowing him to "author" her memoirs.

JAKOBSON, Gregg
DOB: August 2nd
POB: Venice, CA

A songwriter and business associate of record producer Terry Melcher, Jakobson worked for one of Melcher's music publishing companies. Although not an actual member of the Family, Jakobson was intimate with Manson's gang.

JONES, Larry; see Bailey, Lawrence
Page 6

JUAN; see FLYNN, John
Page 31

JUANITA; see WILDEBUSH, Juanita
Page 109

KASABIAN, Linda Darlene Drouin
DOB: 6-21-49
POB: Nashua, New Hampshire
Nickname: Yana the Witch
AKA: Christian, Linda; Chiochios, Linda

In the summer of 1969, the Family welcomed a new female member to its ranks by the name of Linda Kasabian; a nineteen-year-old flower child that had been on her own since she was sixteen. Linda had traveled from the east coast to California during the Summer of Love, wearing the requisite flowers in her hair and along the way consuming vast quantities of psychedelics and experiencing "free love."

On Kasabian's first visit to Spahn Ranch, she experienced a surreal and eerie sexual encounter with Tex Watson in a dark shed. Kasabian later described the encounter as unlike anything she'd ever experienced, as paralysis overtook her body while Tex had his way with her. Originally, Kasabian just intended to visit Spahn's for a couple days, but after being balled by Bobby Beausoleil, Tex Watson, Bruce Davis, Steve Grogan and "Donkey Dan" over a torrid two day span, she returned to her pad in the city, picked up her daughter, Tanya, packed all her belongings—which included a bag of righteous acid tabs, as well as $5,000 she ripped off from her husband—and headed back to the ranch, intent on becoming a Family member.

Later, Kasabian became the star witness when Susan Atkins backed out of her deal with prosecutors. Twenty years old at the time of the Tate/LaBianca murders—Kasabian testified that she didn't take part in the killings, and that her role was limited to waiting in the car. In exchange for her testimony, she recieved immunity.

In 1979, Kasabian remarried and was raising four children in New England and had changed her name to Linda Christian. Linda worked as a waitress until being discovered and afterwards moved to Miami, Florida.

In October 1996, police officers in Tacoma, Washington served a warrant on Linda's daughter, Quana Christian aka "Lady Dangerous." Also present was Linda Kasabian/Christian, now going by the name of Linda Darlene Chiochios. Officers confiscated a small baggie containing rock cocaine and a bundle of cash in a dresser drawer. Also in the room was a .45 caliber semi-automatic handgun, ammunition, electronic scales, and cocaine residue. In a hall closet officers located an A-1 army rifle and in another closet a loaded 30-30 Remington rifle. In Linda's purse a small amount of methamphetamine was discovered.

In recent years, Linda has consented to TV interviews.

KATIE; see KRENWINKEL, Patricia
Page 52

KAUFMAN, Phillip Clark
DOB: 4-26-35
POB: Woodland Hills, CA

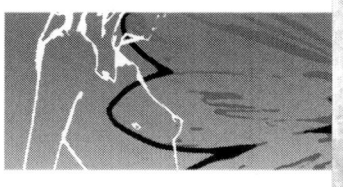

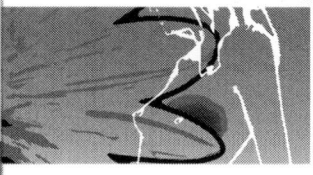

A prison buddy who set up Manson with contacts in the recording industry after his Terminal Island release. When Kaufman got out of the joint, he hooked up with Charlie for a couple of months, enjoying his young girls and dope.

During the Tate-LaBianca trial, Kaufman produced and released Charlie's *LIE* LP. Afterwards, Kaufman gained renown in rock and roll circles as the "Road Mangler" — road manager for such big name acts as The Rolling Stones, Gram Parsons, Emmylou Harris, Joe Cocker, Marianne Faithful and Frank Zappa.

KITTY; see LUTESINGER, Katherine
Page 59

KRENWINKEL, Patricia
DOB: 12-3-47
POB: Los Angeles, CA
Nickname: Katie; Big Patty
AKA: Smith, Cathran Patricia; Reeves, Marnie Kay; Reeves, Kay; Vance, Marina Kay; Kerwinkle, Patricia; Scott, Mary Ann
Prisoner I.D. # W 08314

Eighteen when she met Manson in 1967, Krenwinkel was a former campfire girl, Sunday school teacher and Bible freak, who brought with her a learned background to draw upon when taking in the Biblical babble Charlie later spewed, as she and Manson would quote and counter-quote Bible passages to one another while under the influence of the divine sacrament, LSD.

Pat—as her early diaries noted—was the type of girl the boys seemed to neglect at high school dances. So it should come as no surprise that after spending only four stoned and sex-filled days with Charlie, she quit her job as an insurance company clerk and abandoned her car, leaving her final paycheck behind un-cashed. And though she had turned her back on "The Establishment", Krenwinkel did not entirely swear-off all worldly goods, as she presented her budding family with a valid Chevron credit card backed by her father, who still loved his daughter enough to pay for her gas. Krenwinkel's father later had this to say about the sudden change in his daughter: "I am convinced (Manson) was some kind of hypnotist. It was all so spontaneous."

Krenwinkel was twenty years old when she participated in the Tate-LaBianca murders. For her part, she was convicted on seven counts of first-degree murder and one count of conspiracy to murder. Like the others, she recieved a sentence of death which was later reduced to life.

Currently, Krenwinkel raises and trains dogs for the blind in prison. Of all those convicted for the Tate-LaBianca murders, she has been the most quiet. It is reported that Krenwinkel has great feelings of guilt about her part in the murders and has yet to forgive herself. Like the others, her parole has been continually denied.

LAKE, Diane Elizabeth
DOB: 1953
POB: Minneapolis, MN
Nickname: Snake
AKA: Mak, Diane Elizabeth; Bluestein, Diane Elizabeth

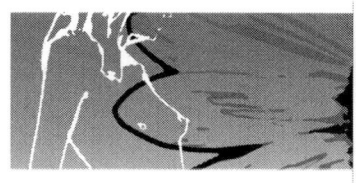

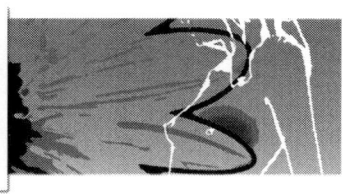

Arrested at the Barker Ranch raid, Diane "Snake" Lake met Manson at the Spiral Staircase house when she was all but fourteen. Diane's parents were part of Wavy Gravy's Hog Farm commune, so the idea of joining Charlie's troupe wasn't such a far-out of an idea, as apparently she'd already experimented with group sex and LSD as a Hog Farm member.

Lake gained her reptilian appellation—as legend goes, via Ed Sander's decorative use of the English language—in "tribute to the transverse ophidian wiggles she made during intercourse." Of all those Manson bedded down, Snake was by far and away Charlie's favorite girl. If any could have laid claim to being Manson's main squeeze, it was the nubile and vivacious Snake, ophidian wiggles and all.

After her Barker Ranch arrest, Lake was held in a psychiatric institution. She was released in August 1970 and testified for the prosecution. According to prosecutor Steven Kay, Lake went to college, got straight A's, married, had children and resides on the

California coast. She became a Born Again Christian and for a time was employed at a bank.

LANE, Robert Ivan
DOB: 4-10-51
Nicknames: Scotty; Soupspoon; Bob
AKA: Davis, Scott Bell

Arrested in the Barker Ranch raid.

LANSBURY, Deidre
Born: Diedre Angela Shaw
DOB: 4-26-1953
Nickname: Didi

One prized acquisition to Manson's pack of pubescent pretties was the daughter of actress Angela Lansbury, Didi. At the time, Didi was only fourteen; so to ward off potential jailbait charges, she carried around with her a to-whom-it-may-concern letter from her mother, OK-ing her association with Manson.

Afterwards, Manson stated that he only met Angela Lansbury briefly on a couple occasions, but that didn't stop Charlie and the crew from taking her credit card down to the local liquor store and purchasing goodies with it.

According to IMDb.com, Angela Lansbury's son—Anthony Pullen Shaw—was also a Manson "follower." After the murders, Lansbury flew Anthony, seventeen at the time, to Ireland to receive help for drug problems.

LEGHORN, Jennifer; see GENTRY, Jennifer Sue

Page 35

LESLIE; see VAN HOUTEN, Leslie

Page 101

LINDA; see KASABIAN, Linda

Page 49

LIPSETT, David William

DOB: 2-9-50/8-3-46
POB: Vallejo, CA
Nicknames: Karate Dave
AKA: Baker, David Ralph; Ellis, Charles; Charley; Lipsick, David

Useful to Charlie to instruct Family members in karate, Lipsett was arrested with Paul Watkins and others in a stolen truck. Boinked Barbara Hoyt. Awaiting trial, he broke out of jail and left the Family.

LITTLE LARRY; see BAILEY, Lawrence

Page 6

LITTLE PATTY; see COTTAGE, Madaline

Page 19

LOVETT, Charles
DOB: 1-3-52
AKA: Chuckleberry, Chuck

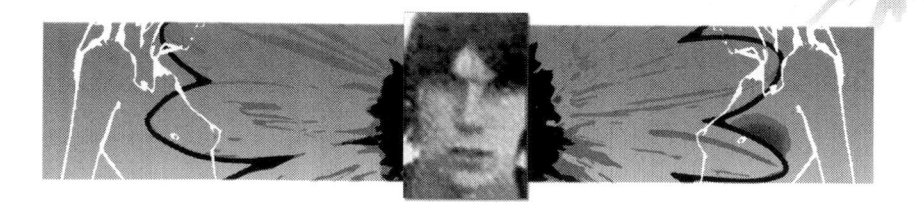

Pictured in *Life* Magazine with the Family in August 1970. Part of the gang that robbed the Western Surplus Store.

LUTESINGER, Katherine Rene
DOB: 8-14-52 or 8-4-50
Nicknames: Kitty; Katie
AKA: Drake, Catherine Lynn

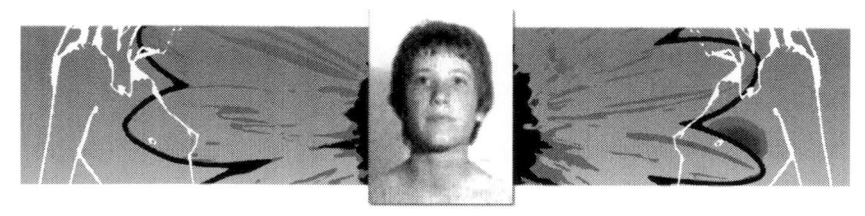

One of Bobby Beausoleil's girlfriends, Lutesinger was seventeen and knocked-up with Bobby's child when she joined the Family. She ran away from the Family at the end of July 1969, and then came back after the murders, the day before the Spahn Ranch raid. Gave birth to Beausoleil's baby on Febraury 11th, 1970. Married Veldon Goucher on January 19th, 1973.

MANSON, Charles Milles

DOB: 11-11-34
POB: Cincinnati, OH
Nicknames: Charlie; Jesus Christ
AKA: Hanson, Charles Willie; Manson, Charles Miller; Milles, Charles Miller; Deer, Charles; Manson, Charles Willis; Maddox, Charles; Summers, Charles Miles; Benson, Charles Miller; Hanson, Charles Willis

Manson's mom, Katherine Maddox, left home in her early teens and gave birth to Charlie at just sixteen, later abandoning him when she came to realize the responsibilities associated with parenthood. Inevitably, Katherine would reunite with Charlie only to dump him off again afterwards. On one occasion, it has been reported, Katherine traded Charlie to a barmaid for a pitcher of beer.

A bastard child, Manson once identified the person who fathered him as "a young drugstore cowboy who called himself Colonel Scott." In 1936, Katherine Maddox sued Colonel Scott for child support, and the court of Boyd County, Kentucky awarded her a lump sum of $25 plus $5 dollars a month for upkeep. Scott defaulted on the judgment and died in 1954 without ever acknowledging Charlie as his son. Katherine later married an older man, William Manson, who was around just long enough to give young Charlie his surname.

Two years after Charlie's birth, Katherine Maddox was arrested when she and her brother, Luther, robbed a service station in West Virginia, knocking out the attendant with a coke bottle. For this offense, Maddox was sentenced to five years in the state pen.

While his mother was behind bars, Manson was shuttled between relatives, orphanages and reformatories. During his mom's many absences, Charlie passed his time developing into a competent thief. Due to these activities, Manson was eventually caught (more than once) and sent away to reform school at nine years of age.

Manson's first stop was the Gibrault School for Boys in Terre Haute, Indiana. Thus began the revolving reformatory door, which Charlie was in and out of over the next several years. By the time he was in his early teens, Manson was living on his own in Indiana, working menial jobs, and supplementing whatever meager income he could generate by common thievery. Again, this inevitably brought him to the attention of the authorities. But this time when Manson was brought before the court, the attending Judge decided to take pity on the lad, arranging for him to be sent to the prestigious Boy's Town U.S.A. Eerily, an Indianapolis newspaper at this time carried a photo of young Charles Milles Manson—decked out in suit and tie—being admitted into Boy's Town, which carried the corny caption: "Boy leaves 'sinful' home for a new life in Boy's Town." This "new life" of Charlie's lasted all of three days, when he ran away from the school.

In April 1949, Manson was committed to the Indiana Boy's

School in Plainfield. After two years there, he was paroled and in short order committed rape on a younger boy. Back at Plainfield, Manson—now eighteen—was listed as "dangerous, with homosexual and assaultive tendencies." In February 1951, he led a gang of six youths in an escape from Plainfield, high-tailing it for California, stealing cars and robbing service stations along the way. This spree of automotive thievery came to a sudden halt just outside of Beaver, Utah, when they hit a police roadblock.

Manson's next stop was the National Training School for Boys in Washington, D.C. During his stint there, Charlie finagled a transfer to the Natural Bridge Honor Camp, a minimum-security institution and was due for a parole hearing in February 1952 when he sodomized another youth while he held a razor to the boy's throat.

Charlie's next stop on the slow boat to damnation was the Federal Reformatory in Petersburg, Virginia, where he arrived on January 18th, 1952. By August he had committed eight serious disciplinary offenses, three of which were violently sexual in nature. Later that year, he was transferred to the Federal Reformatory at Chillicothe, Ohio, where he was granted parole on May 8th, 1954.

Soon after, Manson was arrested for car theft in Los Angeles, as the familiar pattern repeated itself, the revolving door once again opening, and then closing behind him. Convicted, he was sentenced to Terminal Island Prison in San Pedro, California. Manson's stretch at Terminal Island lasted until September 1958, when he was released on five years parole. As soon as Charlie hit the bricks he decided to try his hand at becoming a world class pimp, activities which led to a bench warrant ordered on April 28th, 1959, indicting Manson on Mann Act charges for transporting underage women across state lines. His next stop was McNeil Island, Washington, where he spent five years, until his transfer in June 1966 to Terminal Island. From Terminal Island, Manson was paroled in March 1967, right in time for the Summer of Love.

For Tate/LaBianca, Manson was convicted on seven counts of first-degree murder and one count of conspiracy to commit murder and sent to San Quentin on April 22nd, 1972. He was also convicted of two more first-degree murders for the deaths of Gary Hinman and Donald "Shorty" Shea. Manson originally got the death penalty for the Tate/LaBianca murders. For Hinman/Shea, he was sentenced to life in prison. Manson's death sentence was later changed to "life with the possibility of parole" when California abolished capital punishment.

On October 6th, 1972, Manson was transferred to Folsom Prison. In the fall of 1973, there were reports that he was regressing, and refusing to leave his cell. Taking on a Howard Hughes/hermit-like countenance, Charlie's fingernails grew long and curly, and he was reluctant to bathe. In the view of authorities, Manson's mental state was deteriorating and he was transferred to Vacaville State Prison for psychiatric observation. It wasn't long, though, before Charlie was his old mischievous self, and—in the view of prison officials—had merely feigned mental deterioration as a ploy to get off the Folsom mainline.

In October 1974—when officers at Vacaville found escape

plans outlined in a note written by Manson—he was shipped back to Folsom. The note was discovered during a search of another inmate's cell, and instructed the inmate to tell "them" where Manson was locked up and to find out if "they (can) help us over the fence if we get through the (barred) window." The note also suggested that grenades could "help us blow our way out." The note concluded by asking "if Rainbow was in the North and if the Queen of the South was out of jail?" Investigators suspected that "Rainbow" was a code name for Squeaky and the "Queen of the South" was Sandra Good, who had recently been paroled.

In 1975, Manson maneuvered his way back to Vacaville and was allowed on the mainline again in July 1980, which meant that he could mingle with the general population. Along with Charlie's newfound freedom, he was given the job of chief clerk at the prison chapel. In October 1982, Manson again lost his mainline privileges when a corrections officer tried to enter the chapel and discovered that the office door had been bound from the inside by electrical wire. A more extensive search of the clerk's office revealed a secret trap door leading to the attic. There officers discovered a well-stocked cache, which included a glass vial containing a volatile white liquid, a piece of metal stock sharpened into a weapon, sandpaper, wirecutters, four bags of pot, one hundred feet of nylon cord, and a hot air balloon catalog. A search of Manson's cell later turned up a hacksaw blade, more marijuana, and a quantity of LSD. It was obvious to authorities that Charlie had been planning a prison break, and although the attic was enclosed, it was connected to a series of air ducts, which would have eventually led to freedom.

On September 24th, 1984, inmate Jan Holmstrom doused Charlie with paint thinner and set him on fire in the Vacaville hobby shop. Apparently, Manson had objected to Holmstrom chanting "Hare Krishna," which set off the former Hare Krishna sect member on his paint thinner throwing tirade. Other inmates extinguished the flames and rushed Manson to the prison hospital. Charlie suffered burns over eighteen percent of his body, mainly to the face, hands and scalp, but the injuries were minimal, and did not cause any long lasting negative effects.

In July 1985, Manson was transferred to San Quentin and then later to Corcoran State Prison in March 1989, where for many years he shared a cell next to Sirhan Sirhan. In August of 1997, Manson was caught trafficking drugs and transferred to Pelican Bay Prison on the North Coast of California. Charlie was later returned to the Protective Housing Unit (PHU) at Corcoran on March 26th, 1998, where he has since been interred.

MELCHER, Terry
DOB: 2-8-42
DOD: 12-19-04

Son of actress Doris Day, Melcher was a music producer associated with the Manson Family. In the summer of 1968, Tex Watson attended parties hosted by Melcher and his then girlfriend, Candice Bergen, at 10050 Cielo Drive, where Melcher then lived and which he later subleased to Roman Polanski and Sharon Tate. Former Manson Family member Catherine Share claimed that she and Susan Atkins visited the Cielo Drive address prior to the murders, both swimming in the pool on the grounds. Melcher later confirmed this swimming pool story, and it was revelations such as these that appear to discount the theory that the murders were entirely random.

Beach Boy Dennis Wilson introduced Melcher to Manson in 1968 and was invited to Spahn Ranch to hear Charlie perform. At one time or another, Melcher apparently expressed interest in recording Charlie, but Manson claimed that Melcher welshed on the deal. This led some to suspect that a possible motive for the Tate murders was retaliation aimed at Melcher for failing to champion Charlie's music career, and that Manson's gang was expecting to find the record producer at 10050 Cielo Drive on the night the deed went down. According to author Ed Sanders, the relationship between the Manson Family and Melcher was much more extensive than has ever been admitted and that an "area of silence" had been erected around this association.

MELTON, Charles
POB: Reseda, CA
Nickname: Crazy Charlie (Mentioned in Ed Sander's *The Family*.)

A friend of Bob Kasabian, Linda's husband. Gypsy Share met Linda Kasabian while visiting Melton, and Linda later returned to steal money from him.

MELTON, Larry Allen
Nickname: White Rabbitt

A Haight-Ashbury hippie who visited Spahn Ranch after Charlie's arrest. In the summer of 1998, Melton led Inyo County law enforcement officers to Barker Ranch where he claimed that the bodies of three teenagers—allegedly murdered by Manson and Tex Watson—were buried. Although officers spent several hours digging, no remains were unearthed. Evidence later suggested that Melton had merely cooked up the story about the bodies to garner his obligatory fifteen minutes of fame. Last accounts place him in the Texas State Prison system.

MCCANN, Brenda; see PITMAN, Nancy
Page 77

MONFORT, Michael Lee
DOB: 6-28-48
Deceased
Nickname: Red Eye
AKA: Foote, Gordon

An Aryan Brotherhood member and Manson Family associate in the 1970's. Pled guilty to the murder of Lauren Willett and sentenced to seven years to life. Married Nancy Pitman on January 27th, 1976.

MONTGOMERY, Charles; see WATSON, Charles
Page 108

MOOREHOUSE, Deane Allen
DOB: 2-13-20
AKA: Baba

A former minister and father of Ruth Ann, Moorehouse was turned on to acid by Manson and stayed at Dennis Wilson's house after the Family moved on. Moorehouse and Tex Watson visited Terry Melcher on several occasions at his residence at 10050 Cielo Drive.

Moorehouse went to prison in 1970 for giving LSD to minor girls. He reconnected with the Sacramento Manson girl contingent living there in the mid-70's. According to his ex-wife, Moorehouse was convicted in the late 1980's for molesting his own children. He is listed in the California Sex Offenders database at www.meganslaw.ca.gov.

MOOREHOUSE, Ruth Ann
DOB: 1-6-51
POB: Toronto, Canada
Nickname: Ouisch
AKA: Madison, Rachael; Susan; Morse, Rachael Susan; Heuvelhurst, Ruth Ann; Smith, Ruth Ann

"Ouisch" met Charlie at fourteen when he visited her father in San Jose, California. After running away from her real family and being brought back, she married a bus driver then left him to join Charlie's Family. In September 1970, Moorehouse accompanied Barbara Hoyt to Hawaii and gave her an LSD-laced hamburger. Pregnant and on bail, she fled the state and charges were dropped. Interviewed for Jess Bravin's book, *Squeaky*, Moorehouse is apparently Born Again and has avoided contact with former Family members. She currently works a normal job somewhere in the mid-west.

MORGLEA, Randy J.
DOB: 5-15-51
POB: Thomasville, NC
AKA: Todd, Hugh Rocky

Arrested with the Family in the Barker Ranch raid.

MURRAY, Robert Earl
DOB: 8-8-45
POB: Pittsford, NY

Unknown. Listed in police files.

OUISH/OUISCH; see MOOREHOUSE, Ruth
Page 71

PIERCE, Charles
Nickname: Sunshine

Introduced to the Family by Ella Jo Bailey. Sunshine left the Family at Spahn Ranch in June 1968 after allegedly refusing to participte in a murder for Charlie. Said to have gone to Texas.

PITMAN, Nancy Laura
DOB: 1-1-51
POB: Springfield, IL
Nicknames: Brenda; Malibu Brenda; Penelope; Brindle, Ice
AKA: McCann, Brenda Sue; Brindle, Brenda; Moss, Brenda; Perrell, Cydette; Miller, Penelope Rose; Tracy, Penelope R.; McKay, Brenda Marie

Arrested with the Family at the Barker and Spahn ranch raids. Pitman surrendered with Bruce Davis when he came in for murder charges, and she for forgery, in December 1970. Rumor has it Pitman accompanied Manson and Davis back to the Tate murder scene and rearranged things to leave false clues, possibly moving Sharon Tate's body. Pitman married Mike Monfort, and pled guilty to being an accessory after the fact in the October/November 1972 murder of Lauren Willett, wife of James (also slain), serving a three year sentence.

In 1989, Ed Sanders reported that Pitman was married with three kids, living in Napa, California. She currently resides in Bend, Oregon, and is working as a technical advisor for the forthcoming *Manson Family Girls* movie.

PLUMLEE, Vernon Ray Dean
DOB: 1-11-49 or 2-14-50
POB: Corvallis, OR
Nickname: Vern
AKA: Thompson, Vern Edward; Vitasek, Arnold Edward

Arrested with Family at Spahn Ranch. Plumlee claimed that the motive for the Tate/LaBianca murders involved LSD and that he had "...heard things about something to the effect the LaBiancas were supposed to have sold to 'the Tates,' the Tates were supposed to have sold to the Family, and some people got uptight about it, 'cause it was a burn... Like, I was told by him (Bill Vance), he says,

'...don't worry about it though because they'll never out who did it.' So I just let it slide."

POSTON, Brooks Ramsey
DOB: 12-15-48 or 1951
POB: Boger, TX

Spahn Ranch hand and musician. Deane Moorehouse introduced Poston to the Family at Dennis Wilson's house. As was custom for new recruits to bestow all their worldly goods unto the Church of Charlie, Poston did just that when joining Manson's clan, forking over a credit card belonging to his mother that was used extensively during Manson Family travels in 1968.

Poston and Paul Watkins moved away from the Family into the hills of Death Valley with gold miner/metaphysician Paul Crockett. As legend has it, Poston believed that Charlie was Jesus Christ until "deprogrammed" by Crockett.

During the trial, Poston testified for the prosecution. Afterwards, he formed a band with Paul Watkins called Desert Sun and their music was used in the documentary, *Manson*.

Currently, Poston resides in Louisana.

PUGH, Joel
DOB: 1940
DOD: 1968

Alleged husband of Sandy Good. Pugh traveled to London in late 1968, accompanied by Bruce Davis. On December 1st, 1969, Pugh's decomposing body was discovered in a London Hotel. His throat had been cut with razor blades, there were slash marks on both wrists and his blood had been used to inscribe backwards writing on a mirror in the room. Scotland Yard ruled the death a suicide, although the Inyo County D.A. suspected otherwise.

RAPH, Kevin Schooler
DOB: 8-4-49
POB: Arkansas

Unknown. Arrested with Family members.

RICE, Dennis
DOB: 9-15-39 or 11-2-39
Nickname: Fatherman

Involved in the Western Surplus Store shoot-out. Today, Rice operates Free Indeed Ministries, a nonprofit Christian organization based in Tempe, Arizona.

ROSENBERG, Barbara
DOB: 12-27-47
Nickname: Bo; Rainbow

Suspected as an alias of Barbara Hoyt in Bugliosi's *Helter Skelter*, Paul Watkins said in his book *My Life with Charles Manson* that Barbara Rosenberg and Shelly (Unknown) "...lived with the hippies at Spahn Ranch" prior to the arrivals of the Mansonoids, and distinguishes that Rosenberg had joined the Family well before Hoyt. In the *Manson* documentary, Hoyt is pictured seperate from Rosenberg. In Ed Sanders' *The Family*, Hoyt and Rosenberg are mentioned seperately and at different time periods.

In *The Family*, Sander's recounted an apocryphal tale regarding a Manson Family acid orgy where Bo Rosenberg went crazy while giving Charlie head and bit off his cock. Manson, it is said, miraculously healed his severed member with a magical wave of the hand, and then continued on with the wild drug fueled orgy as if nothing had happened. Hallelujah!

ROSS, Mark Stephen
DOB: 2-27-45
POB: New York

Owned the apartment where "Zero" Haught died. Started hanging around Charlie's Family after the ranch raid arrests. Ross was friend's with Robert Hendrickson, one of the producers of the *Manson* documentary, and this association allowed Hendrickson to film the Manson Family. Ross was arrested with Gypsy Share and Sandra Good for protesting in court the judge's order that Manson not be allowed to represent himself.

ROUGH, Johnny Kevin

Listed in police files. Possibly the unknown "Kevin" mentioned in Paul Watkins' *My Life with Charles Manson*.

ROWE, Stephanie Gale
(Real name may be Suzanne Scott)
DOB: 3-23-50
POB: Los Angeles
AKA: Scott, Suzanne; Junior, Barbara

An early member of the Manson Family.

SADIE; see ATKINS, Susan
Page 2

SANDY; see GOOD, Sandra
Page 36

SCHRAM, Stephanie Jean
DOB: 11-13-50 or 11-13-51
POB: Los Angeles
AKA: Mathews, Carol

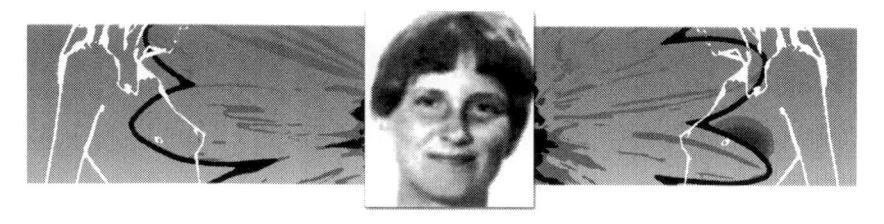

On an August 4th, 1969 road trip to Big Sur, Manson picked up an attractive seventeen-year-old hitchhiker, Stephanie Schram, and later that night on the beach gave Stephanie her first hit of acid, initiating her in a session of LSD sex therapy. "He sure did send me on a trip that one day," Schram later noted.

Schram was arrested in the Spahn Ranch raid. Three days out of jail, she and Manson were busted for marijuana, (although later released when lab tests couldn't prove positive for cannabis) then afterwards returned to her parents. Schram promptly returned to Charlie's Family and later fled Barker Ranch with Kitty Lutesinger. Later, she testified for the prosecution.

In the 1970's Schram operated a dog grooming business.

SCHWARM, Mary Ann
AKA: Von Ahn, Diane

Arrested in the Barker Ranch raid. From Portland, Oregon, Schwarm was introduced into the Family by Bill Vance and Vern Plumlee.

SCOTT, Suzanne; see ROWE, Stephanie
Page 86

SCOTTY; see BROWN, Kenneth
Page 12

SHARE, Catherine Louise
DOB: 12-10-42
POB: France
Nicknames: Cathy; Gypsy
AKA: Wright, Kathleen May; James, Catherine Ann; Manon, Minette; Shore, Diane/Louise; Jessica

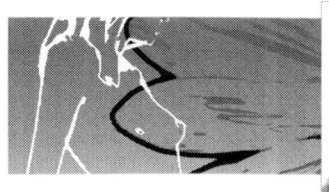

Share was playing a part in a B-movie with Bobby Beausoleil when she joined Bobby's harem of girlfriends that were later absorbed into the Family. She drove Shorty Shea's car to a shopping center after his murder, and has said that Manson Family members were inside the LaBianca house two weeks before the murders. Share also claimed that she and Susan Atkins visited the Tate property while Terry Melcher lived there, and purportedly swam in the pool. Share was in on the Barbara Hoyt hamburger poisoning and wounded with three shots during the Western Surplus Store shootout. Sentenced on August 21st, 1971, she was paroled March 3rd, 1975.

Share married Kenneth Como while he was in prison in 1977 and lived near Folsom with her seven year old son. In 1979, she was indicted by a federal grand jury on six courts of mail fraud, interstate transportation of stolen property and fraudulent credit card use, and was later convicted on federal mail fraud charges.

In the late 1980's, Share was hidden by the Federal Witness

Protection Program due to a former husband (not Kenneth Como) testifying against former associates. During that period, she was rumored to have been living in the southwestern U.S. and Texas. In recent years, Share has resurfaced. Like so many other former Mansonoids, she's become Born Again, and has appeared on TV interviews. According to sources, Share worked for a period of time for an airline.

SHEA, Donald Jerome
DOB: 9-18-33
POB: Boston, MA
Nickname: Shorty

Spahn Ranch hand murdered by Manson Family members on August 25th or 26th, 1969. Manson suspected that the Spahn raid was brought on by Shorty snitching to the heat.

For many years it was believed that several Family members—including Manson, Steve Grogan, Bruce Davis, Bill Vance, Larry Bailey and some of the girls—had tortured Shorty and played mind games with him prior to his murder, and that his body was hacked to pieces, then buried at Spahn Ranch. Legend grew of Shea's murder until it became an apocryphal tale that was embellished upon to ridiculous proportions by Manson Family members. One version had the girls masturbating Shorty, as one of the men lopped off his head at the exact instant he climaxed. This part of the legend was later discredited when Steve Grogan directed authorities in 1977 to the actual whereabouts of Shorty's burial site at Spahn's. Once exhumed, his remains were discovered still intact.

SHEPPARD, Laura Ann
DOB: 4-4-51
POB: Detroit, MI
Nickname: Julia
AKA: Roberts, Julia

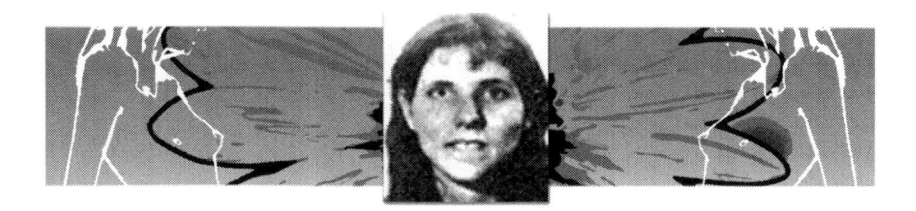

Unknown. Arrested with Family at Spahn Ranch.

SIMI VALLEY SHERRY; see COOPER, Sherry Ann

SINCLAIR, Colleen Ann
DOB: 6-9-49 or 7-11-53
POB: Nevada
AKA: Collie, Beth, Tracy

Arrested with the Family in the Barker Ranch raid.

SINDER, Ella Beth; see BAILEY, Ella Jo
Page 5

SMITH, Claudia Leigh
DOB: 8-11-50
POB: CA
Nickname: Collie
AKA: Andrews, Sherry; Andrews, Claudia; Tracy, Beth

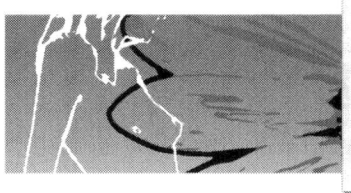

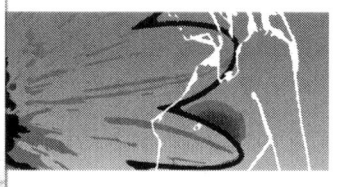

Arrested at the Barker Ranch raid. Was at the Venice apartment when "Zero" Haught died.

SNAKE; see LAKE, Diane

Page 55

SOUPSPOON; see LANE, Robert

Page 56

SQUEAKY; see FROMME, Lynette

Page 32

STEPHANIE; see either SCHRAM, Stephanie;
Page 89
or ROWE, Stephanie

Page 86

TEX; see WATSON, Charles

Page 108

TJ; see WALLEMAN, Tom

Page 105

TODD, Hugh Rocky; see MORGLEA, Randy

Page 71

TOWNSEND, Herb
DOB: 1952

Arrested in the Spahn Ranch raid.

TRACEY, Beth; see SINCLAIR, Colleen

Page 94

TRUE, Harold Irving
DOB: 8-5-40
POB: Los Angeles

A friend of Phil Kaufman, True rented a house at 3267 Waverly Drive in the Los Feliz District of Los Angeles next door to Leno and Rosemary LaBianca's home. According to a member of the district attorney's staff, Charlie and his crew visited the True house in 1968 for "pot and LSD parties."

VAN HOUTEN, Leslie Louise
DOB: 8-23-49/48
POB: Iowa
Nickname: LuLu
AKA: Sankston, Leslie Mary; Owens, Leslie Sue; Alexandria, Louella Maxwell; Alexander, Louise Susan
Prisoner I.D. # W 13378

The freshman class treasurer of her California high school, in June 1968 eighteen year old Leslie met Bobby Beausoleil and eventually wound up at Spahn Ranch. Van Houten was twenty-two when she took part in the LaBianca murders, but was not present the night before at the Tate residence. Van Houten was convicted on two counts of first-degree murder and one count of conspiring to commit murder. She was sentenced to death, but her sentence was later reduced to life.

Leslie won a new trial in 1977. She claims that brainwashing, LSD, and mind control by Manson enabled her to kill. The jury was deadlocked and another trial was scheduled. Released on bail, she worked as a secretary for a lawyer. Van Houten had her third trial in 1978 and was found guilty of first degree murder and sentenced to life.

Married William D. Cywin on November 18th, 1981, who was busted in 1982 on bad check charges and for having a female prison guard's uniform in his possession. Soon after, the two were divorced. Van Houten is currently incarcerated at the California Institute for Women.

VERN; see PLUMLEE, Vernon
Page 78

VON AHN, Diane; see SCHWARM, Mary Ann
Page 90

WALLACE, Kay

Pictured and listed in the 1971 *Manson* documentary.

WALLEMAN, Tom
DOB: 12-18-42
DOD: 6-7-95
Nicknames: T.J. the Terrible
AKA: Alden, Jay Thomas

Walleman lived with a group of hippies at Spahn's before the Manson Family arrived. He drove Charlie to the apartment where Bernard Crowe was shot. Walleman dropped in and out of the Family scene over the years and was killed in an auto accident in 1995.

WALTS, Allen
Nickname: Fats

Manson Family associate who claimed that he and Charlie visited Dean Martin's home and that "Charlie delivered drugs there." He suspected that Manson killed his brother, Mark Walts.

WALTS, Mark
DOB: 1-23-53
DOD: 7-18-69

On July 17th, 1969, sixteen-year-old Mark Walts disappeared while hitchhiking in Chatsworth. His battered body was found in Topanga Canyon the next morning, having been shot three times and ran over repeatedly by a car. Though not a Spahn Ranch hand or member of the Family, Walts was a frequent visitor to the ranch, and the dead boy's brother, Allen Walts, publicly accused Manson of the murder. Although charges were never filed, several police officers visited Spahn Ranch to investigate Walts' death.

WARTHAN, Perry
AKA: Red

In the mid-70's, Perry "Red" Warthan—a member of an Ohio based neo-Nazi outfit called the Universal Order—began exchanging letters with Manson filled with grandiose plans of starting a Nazi/ Mansonoid training camp in the woods near Oroville, California. Manson even went so far as to send Lynette Fromme to check out Warthan, and—having passed the Squeaky-test—Warthan and Manson began face-to-face meetings at Vacaville Prison. This all came to an abrupt end in September 1982 when Warthan murdered a teenaged drifter named Joe Hoover, thus ending Operation Nazi Youth Camp. Authorities say the boy had been slain because he mouthed off to police about Warthan's neo-Nazi group.

WATKINS, Paul Allen
DOB: 1-25-50
POB: Oxnard, CA
DOD: 8-3-90
Nickname: Little Paul

Watkins became a valuable witness in the Tate-LaBianca trial, documenting the Helter Skelter theory of the prosecution's case. He appeared in the *Manson* documentary and co-authored *My Life with Charles Manson*. Before succumbing to leukemia in 1990, Watkins and his wife, Martha, and two daughters, lived in Tecopa, a small desert town near Death Valley. Watkins was founder and first president of the Death Valley Chamber of Commerce, and unofficial mayor of the town. Prior to his death, he lectured extensively on cult psychology and the effects of substance abuse.

WATSON, Charles Denton
DOB: 12/2/45
POB: Dallas, TX
Nicknames: Tex; Mad Charlie; Crazy Charlie
AKA: Watson, Charles Denton Shine, Samuel Lee
Prisoner I.D. # B-37999

Part owner of a wig shop and dating a stewardess, mod-dressed Charles "Tex" Watson met Manson at Dennis Wilson's house and in short order became one of Charlie's head henchmen. On October 2nd, 1969, before the heat came down, Watson fled to Texas to hide out. There he was arrested and eventually extradited to California. While awaiting trial, Tex lost fifty pounds and was unable to communicate or feed himself. He reached an acute state of psychosis and was sent to the Atascadero State Hospital. Once his health improved, Watson was tried, found guilty and sentenced to death. A year later, the Supreme Court abolished the death penalty and Watson's mental instability miraculously improved.

During his imprisonment at the Men's Colony in San Luis Obispo, California, Watson has become a successful jailhouse minister and formed a tax-free organization, Abounding Love Ministries (ALMS) that provides Christian materials to inmates. In 1979, he married Kristin Svege (now divorced) and fathered three children before conjugational visits were outlawed in California.

WILD, Victor Floyd
AKA: Brother Ely
DOB: 9-20-40

Made groovy buckskins for Charlie and his chicks at his leather factory in Santa Barbara. Manson was wearing these very same buckskins when later arrested in Death Valley. Wild was alleged to be the high priest of a clandestine occult group, which the Santa Barbara police believed to be a "chapter" of The Process Church of the Final Judgement.

WILDEBUSH, Joan
DOB: 1-21-44
AKA: Juanita Wildebush

In the summer of '69, another new initiate joined the group by the name of Juanita Wildebush, a last name that brought no lack of giggles to the Manson men, many of whom later "plowed her wild bush." Wildebush—described by Ed Sanders as an "eager young lady with a Rubenesque Frame"—was a schoolteacher on summer vacation, when she picked up four hitchhikers—T.J., Tex, Ella and Clem—near Palo Alto, California. She took the four to San Jose, and they eventually persuaded her to drive them down to Spahn Ranch so that she could meet Charlie. Apparently, it didn't take long for Manson to cast his love-spell. After an all day grope-session, Wildebush withdrew $11,000 from a trust fund set up by her father, and immediately handed it over to Manson. She was later sent with Brooks Poston to live at Barker Ranch before Manson moved his entire Family there.

Wildebush eloped with Bob Berry, Paul Crockett's gold mining partner.

WILLETT, James L.
DOB: 6-14-46
DOD: November, 1972
AKA: James Forsher?

and WILLETT, Lauren Chavelle Olmstead
DOB: 5-17-53
DOD: November, 1972
AKA: Lauren Elder?

James Willett was murdered prior to November 8th, 1972; Lauren was murdered on November 10th or 11th of that same year. The young couple had been hanging with remnants of the post-conviction Manson crowd in Stockton, California. James—a former Marine from Los Angeles—was buried near the Russian River in Northern California. He'd been shot with a shotgun and decapitated. His wife's body was found shot once in the head and buried in the basement of the Stockton house. Vincent Bugliosi suspected that James and Lauren lured Manson Attorney Ronald Hughes to his death at Sespe Hot Springs.

WILSON, Dennis Carl
DOB: 12-4-44
DOD: 12-27-83

Beach Boy Dennis Wilson picked up two hippie chicks one day—Ella Jo Bailey and Patricia Krenwinkel—and took them back to his Sunset Boulevard pad where Manson later showed up with the rest of the Family. Before moving to Spahn Ranch, Manson was a permanent fixture at Wilson's place, but when too many freaky people started showing up, Wilson vacated the premises, letting the lease run out. Nonetheless, they remained friends and Charlie planned to launch his music career with Wilson's help. Dennis bought one of his songs, "Cease to Exist" which The Beach Boys released as "Never Learn Not to Love" on their album *20/20*.

On Christmas day 1983, Wilson died near a yacht owned by a friend docked at Marina Del Rey, California. The official ruling was death by drowning—in all of but twelve feet of water—although little was said about a nasty gash discovered on his forehead. Afterwards, Dennis' wife, Shawn, requested that her husband's remains be buried at sea, a request agreed to by then President Ronald Reagan. Conspiracy researcher Mae Brussell believed that Dennis had been a murder victim, and that the civilian's burial at sea was a clever way of disposing of his body without benefit of a proper autopsy. The cause of Dennis' conjectured murder—Brussell suspected—was due to knowledge he possessed of famous V.I.P videotapes discovered at 10050 Cielo Drive after the murders. Brussell contended that the Tate-LaBianca murders—including Wilson's death—were part a massive cover-up reaching far and wide, beginning with the LAPD and going all the way to the highest levels of government. In a 1976 interview, Wilson said, "I know why Manson did what he did. Someday I'll tell the world. I'll write a book and explain why he did it." Unfortunately, Wilson never had a chance to write his book.

YELLER; see Bailey, Ella Jo

Page 5

ZERO; see HAUGHT, John
Page 42

About the Authors

Adam Gorightly

A certified "crackpot historian" and 23rd degree Discordian, Adam Gorightly has been chronicling fringe and conspiracy culture in an illuminating manner for over two decades. An active contributor to the 'zine revolution of the late '80s and early '90s, Adam's byline was a familiar sight in many cutting-edge magazines of the period where he sharpened his literary teeth. His articles have appeared in numerous publications such as *The Excluded Middle*, *UFO Magazine*, *Paranoia*, *SteamShovel Press*, and *FourTwoFour*, the largest soccer magazine in Great Britain.

Adam's explorations into these arcane waters eventually led to his first book, published in October 2001, *The Shadow Over Santa Susana: Black Magic, Mind Control and the Manson Family Mythos*, which has been described as the mother of all Manson family tomes. This was followed in November 2003 by *The Prankster and the Conspiracy: The Story of Kerry Thornley and How He Met Oswald and Inspired the Counterculture*, the first biography of the legendary counterculture figure, chronicling Thornley's amazing and tragic life. 2005's *The Beast of Adam Gorightly: Collected Rantings 1992–2004*, features many articles from Adam's formative years in the 'zine scene. Before *A Who's Who of the Manson Family*, he authored *James Shelby Downard's Mystical War* which chronicles the famed conspiracy researcher's life long battles against Masonic Sorcery.

Contact Adam at your own risk at adamgorightly.com or adamgorightly@yahoo.com.

Shamus McFarland

Little is known about Shamus McFarland other than his artistic ability as demonstrated by his talents displayed on the front and back covers of *A Who's Who of the Mason Family*. He remains to Feejee Press and others a mystery figure of immense talent. We thank him for his efforts in compiling this must-read book on the Manson Family members and other associated folk.

Companion Soundtrack

Michael Montes

Dark, terrifying, disturbing, and yet Sexy Sadie can dance to it.

To enhance your print and Amazon Kindle reading experience of *A Who's Who of the Manson Family* composer Michael Montes has carefully compiled 7 of his most hauntingly surreal works for

A Who's Who of the Manson Family: A Companion Soundtrack to the Book

Now as you read, this Companion Soundtrack by acclaimed composer Michael Montes will add another dimension to the psychotic deeds and horrible crimes of the Manson Family members with incredible music.

Purchase for download this great music now from
http://www.feejeepress.com/whoswhomansonsoundtrack/

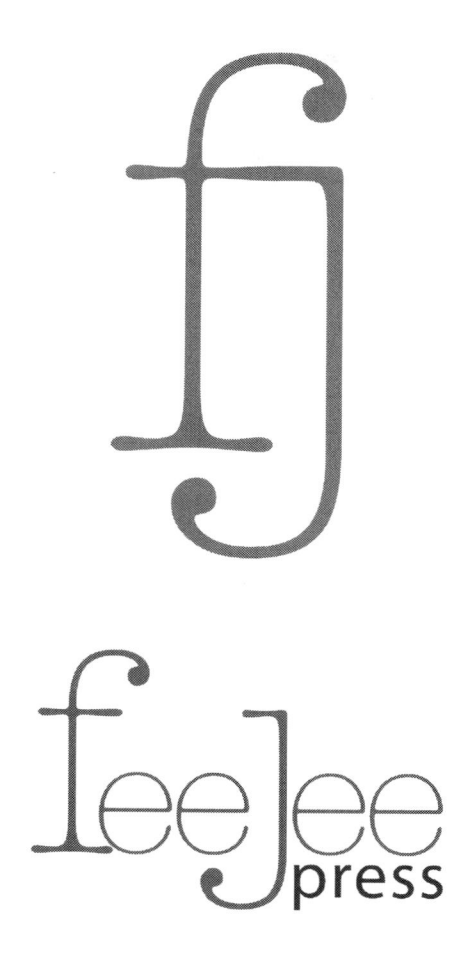

This book also available on Amazon Kindle.
Visit feejeepress.com to learn more.

Printed in Great Britain
by Amazon.co.uk, Ltd.,
Marston Gate.